GLOBAL ENGLISH
READ & WRITE SOUND METHOD
R R S M

- Learn in less than one hour

- Write words as they sound

- Teach ESL students easily

- Spelling is simplified

- Pronunciation is effortless

- Global writing with English

Beyond mere phonetics, learn a simple, foolproof, and common sense methodology for reading and writing the most widely used language on Earth: English

Khosrow Javaherian

iUniverse, Inc.
New York Bloomington

iUniverse books may be ordered through booksellers or by contacting:

iUniverse
1663 Liberty Drive
Bloomington, IN 47403
www.iuniverse.com
1-800-Authors (1-800-288-4677)

ISBN: 978-1-4502-3030-8 (sc)
ISBN: 978-1-4502-3031-5 (ebook)

Printed in the United States of America

iUniverse rev. date: 08/04/2010

PREFACE

Through forty years of travels and experience working with different cultures as an American civil engineer, I have come to understand that communicating in written English is a major universal tool, despite all its complexities and irregularities.

The purpose of this book is to simplify, regulate, and henceforth upgrade the quality of the English reading and writing system to assist in the globalization of the English language.

The adoption of a new system is not unprecedented. English-speaking countries implemented the logical universal metric measurement only a few decades ago to benefit the English educational system. Today the metric system is partially used as an alternate system in English societies and may require another decade to obtain close to full usage.

The Read and Write Sound Method (RRSM) presented in this book is derived from various advanced Latin alphabet writing systems of past decades in conjunction with common sense methodology that would prove beneficial for the English language. The approach outlined in this book is intended to "get to the point." It is an approach that readers can easily understand and implement.

Today's generation of English speakers is more receptive to adopting logical innovations in lieu of following complex traditional rules that encouraged me to write this book.

Khosrow Javaherian

Contents

PART 1

INTRODUCTION

Throughout world history, languages have evolved and have become increasingly systematic. For example a well-structured auxiliary language called Esperanto was created in 1905 in Europe. This language's purpose was to internationalize speaking, reading, and writing for all people. Though this system had some degree of success, it did not take hold as intended.

The next significant change occurred in 1928, when Turkey replaced its complex Arabic writing system with an expertly assembled Latin alphabet writing system. As a result, the literacy rate increased from approximately 20 percent to an astonishing 70 percent in merely two years. In 1992, this system was adopted by a former state of Russia, Azerbaijan; the basic concept of the system was to read and write the language as it was pronounced. More recently there have been movements by other states to convert to this system also. This book was influenced by these concepts to upgrade systems of English reading and writing, but not to replace them.

In the twenty-first century, English writing which utilizes the Latin alphabet can be considered a universal writing system despite its various complexities and irregularities. English is considered complex because about 70 percent of written words are not spelled as they are pronounced. In comparison, only approximately 20 percent of the words in the Spanish language are not written as pronounced, however, better than French that falls into a 90 percent range.

For example, compare these two sentences:

1. Barbara rented seven apartments in Oregon.
2. George bought eight science books in Knoxville.

Anyone who is familiar with the Latin alphabet can easily read the first sentence because it sounds as it is written. However, one cannot properly read the second sentence without completing years of schooling. Within an hour of instruction, RRSM will illustrate how the second sentence can be written and read as easily as the first.

See the following simplified example of the second sentence using the Read and Write Sound Method:

Jorj bot eyt sayens buks in Naxvil.

The spelling of words is considerably simplified and there is practically no dependency upon pronunciation guidelines such as complicated phonetic symbols shown in dictionaries after each word.

Regular English	+	Dictionaries (Phonetic)	=	Presented English RRSM
school		skül		skul
educate		e-jə_kāt		ejukeyt
success		sək- ＼ ses		sakses

Implementing English RRSM for other languages has two major benefits. First, teaching English reading and writing to non-English speakers will be considerably easier. Second, replacing non-English language reading and writing systems with the presented English will improve universal communication.

In conclusion, the purpose of this book is to teach common sense simplifications to upgrade English reading and writing systems to a universal level. By modifying words to create close to 100 percent phonetic spelling, RRSM offers a promising alternate English reading and writing method for all levels of the English educational system.

INTENT

The intent of this book is as follows:

- Teach reading and writing of the English language within an hour of instruction by using the Latin alphabet phonetic approach, making it unnecessary to follow several years of complex and irregular schooling rules.

- Simplify word spelling to closely follow phonetic pronunciations.

- Eliminate complex phonetic guideline symbols as those shown in dictionaries.

- Assist in the reading and writing of papers, e-mails, and text messages with spelling simplifications.

- Facilitate the teaching of English as a second language by having words spelled as they are pronounced.

- Teach the reading and writing of other languages by using the English Latin alphabet with minor modifications, which will be close in sound to the intended languages.

- Implement RRSM into all levels of the English educational system.

This book is not intended to accomplish the following:

- Teach language translation.

- Teach the speaking of a new language other than facilitating reading and writing by an alternate method.

- Change the grammar structure of any language other than reading and writing by an alternate method.

- Alter the English dialects other than using close to Standard American dialects for presentation.

Frequently Asked Questions - FAQ

1. I am a native English speaker. What will/can this book teach me?

   - Upgrade your English to a universal level that is almost entirely written as it sounds for future use without dependency on dictionary phonetic alphabets.
   - Read and write other languages you know with presented RRSM rules by using the Latin alphabet.
   - English speakers can teach ESL students reading and writing by RRSM method to assist their learning with dramatic spelling simplifications based on pronunciation.

2. Is this book easy to understand if English is not my first language? Will there be any setbacks if English is not my first language?

   - If one has a rudimentary understanding of the English language, the acquisition of the RRSM will simplify learning English.
   - If a student is not familiar with the English language, one will need the assistance to acquire both English and the RRSM.

3. Will this book alone be enough to teach me how to speak a foreign language correctly?

   - No, speaking a new language requires intensive study; when related to reading and writing, this book can assist in that study.

4. What are some of the irregular English spelling and pronunciation rules that do not come naturally to native English speakers?

   - art, ash, ace (three different sounds for *a*)
   - iron, big, his (three differing sounds for *i*)
   - upon, united, ultra (three differing sounds for *u*)
   - cell, cat, account, access (multiple sounds for *c*)
   - <u>k</u>not, <u>wr</u>ong, ei<u>gh</u>t, <u>gh</u>ost (soundless letters)
   - p<u>ear</u>l, s<u>ur</u>f, h<u>er</u>, b<u>or</u>n, d<u>ir</u>t (same sound many different letters)

HOW TO BENEFIT FROM THIS BOOK

To benefit from this book, the reader should approach RRSM in three steps:

Step 1: Upgrade English reading and writing

- Study *Rules* with guideline pages and use it as a reference tool; memorization is not necessary.

- Follow *English Usage Example 1,* and test yourself as suggested in order to become familiar with the concept.

- Review a few more examples—the more the better to thoroughly familiarize you with application of RRSM.

> Result: Within one hour, the learner is familiar with RRSM.
> Within a few hours to a couple of days, the learner will have mastered usage.

Step 2: To read and write your first language with the English alphabet

- Accomplish Step 1

- Review any Latin-based and non-Latin language usage examples; provide modifications as suggested.

Result: Universal communication will be easier with RRSM because English and the adoption of Latin alphabet is a common goal among the globalizing world.

Step 3: Teach reading and writing English to ESL students.

- Accomplish Step 1

- Teach use of *Rules* to simplify traditional spelling in order to facilitate speaking. No need to go over the guidelines and English usage example pages, because these pages were intended for persons with some basic English knowledge.

Result: Considerably expedited teaching method for English reading and writing.

PART 2

Notes

RULES

READ & WRITE SOUND METHOD

Based on the widely used Latin alphabet for English language which regulated to a universal level that could be implemented to replace other languages reading and writing system. The basic premise of RRSM is very simple and can be learned within an hour: the letters are **always** read or written as they sound using the following rules.

VOWELS:		REMARKS :
A, a	Art, Bar, Tar, Apartment, Barbara	When *A* in a word sounds *EY*, use *Ey / ey* like:
		Taste (Teyst), Potato (Poteyto), Plate (Pleyt)
À, à	At (Àt), Bat (Bàt), Ash (Àsh)	
E, e	End, Edward, Eskimo, Enter, Enjoy	
I, i	Bit, Debit, Big, Tulip, it, Dentist	When *I* in a word sounds *AY*, use *Ay / ay* like: Iron (Ayron), Item (Aytem), Irish (Ayrish)
Ì, ì	Beet (Bìt), Eat (Ìt), Deep (Dìp)	
	Equal (Ìqual), Jean (Jìn), Bee (Bì)	
O, o	Post, Order, October, Port, Over	
Ò, ò	Turf (Tòrf), Her (Hòr), Pearl (Pòrl) Early (Òrli), Surfing (Sòrfing)	Comes from Swedish **Ö** that is pronounced but not identified in English alphabet.
U, u	School (Skul), Tulip, Pull, Rule	When *U* in a word sounds *YU*, use *YU / yu* like: Uniform (Yuniform), United (Yunited)
Ú, ú	Put (Pút), Púsh	*U* also used to abreviate names like: US, UK, UN

CONSONANTS:

B, D, F, H, K, L, M, N, P, Q, R, S, T, W, X, Y, Z, CH, SH, TH, b, d, f, h, k, l, m, n, p, q, r, s, t, w, x, y, z, ch, sh, th		They sound like The English alphabet sounds
C, c	Center (Senter), Cinema (Sinema), Car (Kar), Clay (Klay), Clever (Klever)	Use *S* and *K* in place of *C*
J, j	Jim, Enjoy, Jet, Jenifer, Jar	J also used as French soft J like: Treasure (Trejur), Patronage (Patronaj)
G, g	Garden, English, Gold, Big, Gift	

Notes

RRSM Guidlines

Implementing RRSM rules will regulate <u>English word types</u> shown here, resulting in a universal level to which close to 100 percent of words are written as they sound.

Eliminate from

<u>English word type</u>	<u>Example of words (RRSM shown in parenthesis)</u>
Soundless *H*	Where (Wer), Ghost (Gost), White (Wayt)
Soundless *K*	Knowledge (Nawlej), Knoxville (Naxvil), Knot (Nat)
Soundless *E*	Some (Sam), Prime (Praym), Gate (Geyt),
Soundless *W*	Write (Rayt), Wrong (Rong), Wreck (Rek)
Soundless *GH* or *DG*	Night (Nayt), Ridge (Rij), Knowledge (Nawlej)
A sounds like *E* or *Ey*	An Eskimo (En Eskimo), A plate (Ey plate)
E or *EA* sounds like *I* or *Ì*	The (Thi), Eleven (Ìleven), East (Ìst)
J sounds like *H*	Baja (Baha), San Jose (Sàn Hoze)
S sounds like *Z*	Is (Iz), These (Thiz), Desert (Dezert), Ours (Awrz)
T sounds like *CH* or *SH*	Notation (Notayshin), Actual (Àkchual)
U or *O* sounds like *A*	Up (Ap), Under (Ander), Bundle (Bandl), Top (Tap)
X sounds like *Z*	Xylophone (Zilofon), Xavier (Zaviyer), Xenia (Zenia)
PH sounds like *F*	Philosophy (Filosofi), Pharmaci (Farmasi)
CH sounds like *K*	Chronic (Kronik), Christopher (Kristofer)
Double consonants	Wall (Wal), Office (Afis), Arrange (Àranj)
Double or Multiple vowels	Rain (Reyn), Eat (Ìt), Book (Buk), Cloud (Clawd)
(Unless each pronounced)	Beautiful (Bìyutiful), React (Rìàkt), Deep (Díp)

Note; *Y* and *W* are extensively used to produce the right sound to eliminate double vowels or multiple letters.

<u>Maintain Letters</u>	<u>Non-English words examples used in English</u>
AA Non-English sound	Aalst , Saab—Closer to *A* sound for English
KH Non-English sound	Khaki , Kharkov—Closer to *H* sound for English
GH Non-English sound	Afghani , Baghdad – Closer to *G* sound for English

Notes

To familiarize yourself start with a few simple underlined word changes:

ONE	TWO	THREE	FOUR	FIVE	SIX	SEVEN	EIGHT	NINE	TEN	ELEVEN	TWELVE	THIRTEEN
UAN	**TU**	**THRÌ**	**FOR**	**FAYV**	SIX	SEVEN	**EYT**	**NAYN**	TEN	**ÌLEVEN**	**TUELV**	**THÒRTÌN**

I	YOU	HE	SHE	THEY	ME	US	THEM	HIS	HER	THEIR	OURS	THIS	THOSE	TO	IS	FROM
AY	**YU**	**HI**	**SHÌ**	THEY	**MI**	**AS**	THEM	**HIZ**	**HÒR**	**THEYR**	**AWRZ**	THIS	**THOZ**	**TU**	**IZ**	**FRAM**

Next, take an article from a publication and go over it with RRSM concept that a sample shown here:

This kind of practice will eventually help you master the concept.

Nevada

Thi entàyr steyt ov   iz nown a'z
The entire state of Nevada is known as Indian
Teritori a'nd   Neytiv pipols   ha'v
Territory, and no wonder. Native peoples have
dweled   thi steyt's valiz dezertz a'nd mowntens
dwelled in the state's valleys, deserts and mountains
thowzendz ov yirz.
for thousands of years.

Mach ov   luks jast a'z   wen thi
Much of Nevada looks just as it did when the
payonirz traveld   mor   ey senturi   Thi
pioneers traveled west more than a century ago. The
onli adishin tu thi mostli ancheyngd la'ndskeyp ar
only addition to the mostly unchanged landscape are
thi traylz   kriskros   thi topografi a'nd a'fer
the trails that crisscross the topography and offer
kawntles oportunitiz   tu   awt a'nd explor thi
countless opportunities to get out and explore the
rejan   iz   Trayls a'nd drawz apon
region. This is Nevada Silver Trails, and it draws upon
thi a'dventorus   kamon tu ol ma'nkaynd
the adventurous spirit common to all mankind. cont.

23

Notes

Nevada means "snow-covered" in Spanish, and with
mins *kavered*

more than 30 feet of snow annually in some of the
mor *fit* *anuali* *sam ov*

state's 314 mountain ranges, it delivers.
steyt's *mowntan reynjas*

You won't find much traffic as you drive over the
Yu *faynd mach trafik az Yu drayv*

mountain passes and across the sagebrush-covered
mowntan pa'ses *ekras* *seygbrash kovered*

valleys of Nevada's north central region. In fact, U.S.
va'liz *sentral rijan* *fa'kt*

50 from Fernley to Ely is known as "The Loneliest
Fernli *Eli* *iz nown az Thi Lonliest*

Road in America," so designated by Life magazine
Rod *Amerika* *dezigneyted bay Layf ma'gazin*

more than 20 years ago.
mor *Yirz*

Strap on your hat and pull on your boots for a visit to
Stra'p *yur ha't and pul* *yur buts* *ey* *tu*

northern Nevada's Cowboy Country, where jeans are
z Cawboy Kantri *wer* *Jins* *ar*

the fashion norm and nobody stands on ceremony. In
thi fa'shin *a'nd nobadi* *seremoni*

this region, Old West hospitality is the rule.
ri'jan *hospitaliti iz thi rul*

"America's Adventure Place" is how some describe
Amerika's Advenchur pleys iz *sam diskrayb*

the Reno-Tahoe area. That said, you'll find plenty of
thi Rino-Taho eyria *sed yu'l faynd* *ov*

action in Nevada's westernmost territory.
a'kshin *z* *teritori*

Notes

RRSM - ENGLISH USAGE - EXAMPLE 2

Regular English Spelling

California

The allure of the Golden State must be powerful:
More than 55 million people
can't be wrong. Abundant resources,
some of the nation's most agreeable
landscape go a long way toward explaining
the attraction. Most Americans who
have never set foot west of the Rockies
have heard of the Yosemite Valley,
Palm Springs, Big Sur, Death Valley,
the Golden Gate Bridge, the San Diego
Zoo, and L.A.'s Getty Center. Thanks to
Hollywood movies and TV shows,
California and all its associations—surfing,
sun, starlets lounging by pools,
environmentalists chaining themselves to
condemned trees, urban sprawl, pollution, and
earthquakes— have all entered the popular
imagination.

RRSM spelling

Kalifornya

Thi alur ov thi Golden Steyt mast bi pawerful:
Mor thàn 55 milyun pipol
càn't bì rong. Abandent risorsis,
sam ov thi neyshin'z most àgriàbol
làndskeypz go ey long wey tuward expleyn-
ing thi àtràkshin. Most Amerikànz hu
hàv never set fut west ov thi Rakiz
hav hòrd of thi Yosemiti Vàli,
Palm Springz, Big Sòr, Deth Vàli,
thi Golden Geyt Brij, thi Sàn Diego
Zu, ànd L.A.'z Geti Senter. Thànkz tu
Haliwud muviz ànd TV showz,
Kalifornya ànd ol itz asosieyshinz--sòrfing,
san, starletz lawnjing bay pulz,
envayromentalistz cheyning themselvz tu
kandemd triz, òrben spral, polushin, ànd
òrthqueykz-- hav al enterd thi papular
imajineyshin.

Notes

RRSM - ENGLISH USAGE - EXAMPLE 3

Regular English spelling

RRSM spelling

Cabo San Lucas

Kabo Sàn Lukas

Due to geographic isolation from the Mexican mainland and a tourism infrastructure with close ties to California and other Western states, there is a more pronounced "north of the border" sensibility here than at other Mexican resorts. American cars, products, and dollars are all highly visible, but Los Cabos also has a by-the-seaside feel that is distinctly Mexican, aided immeasurably by the unspoiled grandeur of its desert setting.

Dyu tu jiografik aysoleyshin fram thi Mexikan meynlànd ànd ey turizm infrastrakchur with kloz tayz tu Kalifornya ànd ather Western steytz, ther iz ey mor pronawnsd "north ov thi border" sensibiliti hir thàn àt other Mexikan rezortz. Amerikàn karz, prodaktz, ànd dolarz ar ol hayli vizibol, bat Los Kabos olso hàz ey bay-thi-sisayd fil thàt iz dìstinktli Mexikan, eyded imejurubli bay thi anspoyld grandur ov itz dezert seting.

Notes

RRSM - ENGLISH USAGE - EXAMPLE 4

Regular English spelling

RRSM spelling

The Enjoyment of Music

Responding to music is the most natural thing
in the world, to judge from the multitudes
who sing, dance, hum, whistle, nod, and tap.
Understanding music would seem to be a more
complicated affair, to judge from the endless
books and lectures that attempt to clarify its
meaning to respond to music is to feel its
pervading charm. To understand music is to
perceive its underlying unity.

Thi Enjoyment ov Myuzik

Rispanding tu myuzik iz thi most nàchural thing
ìn thi world, tu jaj from thi maltitudz
hu sing, dans, ham, wisel, nod, ànd tàp.
Anderstánding myuzik wud sim tu bi ey mor
komplikeyted efeyr, tu jaj from thi endles
buks ànd lekshurz thàt atempt tu klàrifay
itz mining tu rispand tu myuzik iz tu fil itz
perveyding charm. Tu anderstánd myuzik iz tu
persiv itz anderlaying yuniti.

Notes

RRSM · ENGLISH USAGE · EXAMPLE 5

<u>Regular English spelling</u>

<u>RRSM spelling</u>

<u>Well, at least the plate was blue</u>

<u>Wel, àt list thi playt waz blu</u>

I often wonder why there is no blue food.
Every other color is well represented in the
food kingdom: corn is yellow, spinach is
green, carrots are orange, raspberries are red,
grapes are purple, mushrooms are brown. So
where is the blue food? And don't bother me
with blueberries; they are purple. The same is
true for blue corn and blue potatoes. They are
purple. Blue cheese? Nice try. It is actually
white cheese with blue mold. Occasionally,
you might run across some blue Jell-O in a
cafeteria. Don't eat it. It wasn't supposed to
be blue. Something went wrong.

Ay ofen wander way ther iz no blu fud.
Evri ather kalor iz wel reprezented in thi
fud kingdam: korn iz yelow, spinach iz
grin, kàrotz ar orenj, rasberiz ar red,
grayps ar pòrpol, mashrumz ar brawn . So
wer iz thi blu fud? Ànd don't bather mi
with bluberiz; they ar pòrpol. Thi seym iz
tru for blu korn and blu poteytoz. They ar
pòrpol. Blu chiz? Nays tray. It iz àkchuali
wayt chiz with blu mold. Okeyjionali,
yu mayt ran ekras sam blu Jell-O in ey
kàfeteria. Don't ìt it. It waz'nt sapozed to
bì blu. Samthing went rong.

Notes

RRSM - ENGLISH USAGE - EXAMPLE 6

<u>Regular English spelling</u>

<u>RRSM spelling</u>

<u>More Wilderness</u>

Once you travel beyond the sprawling exurbs of America, you'll find plenty of open space and peaceful forests. Many of the prairies and woodlands cleared by settlers have returned now that the land is no longer needed for agriculture. In recent decades, America has gained 70 million acres of wilderness, which is more than all the land currently occupied by cities, suburbs, and exurbs, according to Peter Huber, a fellow at the Manhattan Institute. And more people than ever can get to that wilderness because of a technology that we now routinely curse ...

<u>Mor Wildernes</u>

Uans yu travel biyond thi sprawling exurbz ov Amerika, yu'l faynd plenti ov open speys ànd pisful forestz. Meni ov thi práyriz ànd wudlàndz klird bay setlerz hàv ritòrnd now thàt thi lànd iz no longer nìded for agrikulchur. In resent dekeydz, Amerika hàz geynd 70 milyun eykerz ov wildernes, wich iz mor thàn al thi lànd kurentli okupayd bay sìtiz, sabòrbz, ànd exurbz, àkording tu Piter Hyuber, ey felow àt thi Mànhàtàn Institut. Ànd mor pipol tha'n ever kàn get tu thàt wildernes bikoz ov ey teknoloji thàt we naw rutinli kòrs…

Notes

RRSM · ENGLISH USAGE · EXAMPLE 7

Regular English spelling

RRSM spelling

The Modern Automobile

Thi Modern Otomobil

Granted, cars emit greenhouse gases and
create maddening traffic jams, but consider
what else they do. Compared with the models on
the road in 1970, today's cars burn less gasoline
per mile and emit 98 percent fewer pollutants.
That's why, despite the doubling number of cars,
there's much less smog in the air.

Granted, karz emit grinhaws gàsez ànd
krieyt màdening tràfik jàmz, but konsider
wat els they do. Kompayrd with thi madels on
thi rod in 1970, tudey'z karz bòrn les gàsolin
pòr mayl ànd emit 98 pòrsent fyuver polutàntz.
Thàt'z way, dispayt thi dabling namber ov karz,
ther'z mach les smag in thi eyr.

The basic sedan today offers more creature
comforts and safety than the luxury cars of old.
The fatality rate has declined sharply, and cars
have become so reliable that it's rare to come
upon that once-routine sight on the shoulder
of the road: a driver forlornly staring under the
hood.

Thi beysik sidàn tudey aferz mor krichur
kamfortz a'nd seyfti thàn thi luxuri karz ov old.
Thi feytàliti reyt hàz diklaynd sharpli, ànd karz
ha'v bikam so rilaybul thàt it'z reyr tu kam
apan thàt uans-rutin sayt on thi sholder
ov thi rod: ey drayver forlornli stàring ander thi
hud.

Notes

RRSM

FOR

NON-ENGLISH USAGE GUIDELINES

It is becoming more popular among the new generation of the non-English-speaking world to write its own language in accordance with English alphabet rules for ease in communication considering some degree of <u>approximate</u> pronunciations. As examples, some forms of English are:

Spanglish (Spanish English), Japlish (Japanese English), Hinglish (Hindu English), Fingilish (Farsi English), and Chinglish (Chinese English).

The presented English RRSM will improve this task for those who have some basic knowledge of English and the applicable language.

The scope of this book does not allow usage examples for all languages but provides English RRSM usage for two Latin (Spanish and French) and two non-Latin (Japanese and Farsi) languages. The usage for other languages requires similar approach, and one can identify the required modifications for a different language and implement it with English RRSM rules.

Notes

RRSM

FOR

SPANISH USAGE GUIDELINES

It is becoming more popular among the new generation of the Spanish speaking to write its own language in accordance with English alphabet rules for ease in communication considering some degree of <u>approximate</u> pronunciations.

The presented English RRSM will improve this task for those who have some basic knowledge of English and Spanish languages.

Spanish is one of the simplest Latin languages; around 80 percent of words sound as they are written in comparison to English (30 percent) and French (10 percent).

In order to use English RRSM for Spanish language, one should consider the following basic modifications and eliminate the following conventions in Spanish writing:

- *J* as it becomes *H*
- *H* when it is not replaced by *J*
- *V* as it becomes *B*
- *Y* when it stands by itself as it becomes *I*
- *LL* as it becomes *Y*
- *Q* as it becomes *K*
- *UE, UA, AU* as it becomes *WEY, WA, OW*
- *I* as it becomes *Y* when combined with other vowels
- *CC* as it becomes *SK*
- Ñ as it becomes *NY*
- All pronunciation accents on letters

The follow-up example demonstrates how easy it is to implement English RRSM in Spanish.

Notes

i detayada   Onseaba
La historia del tenis es muy larga y detallada. Empieza en la Onceava

fransesa   monhes key
centuria francesa de los monjes que usaban sus manos para pegar a la

echa   kordeha kon kuero ensima   kuerda
pelota hecha de madera o de cordaje con cuero por encima de una cuerda

atrabes   key
atada atraves del patio. Algunos tambien pensaban que la historia del

abia   Gresia
tenis habia empezado antes de esto, en Grecia o en el Egipto antiguo. Es

key kada sivilizasion   tubiese yuego parasido
posible que cada civilizacion pasada tuviese un juego parecido al tenis.

franseses   akreditasion   presioso
Los franceses tienen la mayoria de acreditacion debido a su precioso

lenguhe   key
lenguaje. En realidad, "tenis" vino del verbo *Tenez*, que se usaba "estoy

sakar
listo a sacar".

Translation

The history of tennis is a long and storied tale. It begins with 11th century French monks using their hands to hit a ball made of wood or string wrapped in leather over a rope strung across a courtyard. Some even think that the history of tennis may have started well before that, in Greece or in ancient Egypt. It's possible though, that every early civilization had a game that resembled tennis. The French get most of the credit possibly because of their beautiful language. In fact, "tennis" comes from the French verb *tenez*, which when used to "i'm about to serve."

43

Notes

RRSM

FOR

FRENCH USAGE GUIDLINES

It is becoming more popular among the new generation of the non-English-speaking world to write its own language with English alphabet rules for ease in communication considering some degree of <u>approximate</u> pronunciations.

The presented English RRSM will improve this task for those who have some basic knowledge of English and French languages.

French, more than English, is loaded with complexities but of a different kind. Around 10 percent of words sound as written compared to English (30 percent) and Spanish (80 percent).

In order to use English RRSM, one must consider a few basic modifications for French writing:

Eliminate *CH* as it becomes *SH*

Eliminate *LL* as it becomes *Y*

Eliminate pronunciation accents on letters

Eliminate double or multiple vowels

J is always soft *J* and the English *J* sound becomes *DJ*

Listing all other basic modifications similar to the Spanish guidelines shown is not practical for French language because of excessive sounds rules. However, the following example demonstrates that despite of complex French sound rules, English RRSM usage can be implemented to facilitate French pronunciations.

Notes

Lo' matan per traviyi o buro mer rest
Le lundi matin, mon père travaille au bureau, ma mère reste

a mazon petit sur a lekol e jo' ve a luniversite
à la maison, ma petite sœur va à l'école, et je vais à l'université.

Lo' lo' merkredi lo' jo'di e finalmant lo' vandredi nu
Le mardi, le mercredi, le jeudi, et finalement le vendredi, nous

fezon mem shoz Me lo' wikend e asse diferan
faisons la même chose. Mais le week-end, il est assez différent.

Pandan lo' wikend nu no' som pa tre okupe com
Pendant le week-end, nous ne sommes pas très occupés comme

le otre jur Lo' samdi mo'tan per ki e tre
les autres jours. Le samedi matin, mon père qui est très sportif

fe do' na'ta'sion e mer fe kwizin pars ke shak
fait de la natation, et ma mère fait la cuisine parce que chaque

samdi me pa'ran invitan tant a diner avek nu Anfln
samedi, mes parents invitent ma tante à dîner avec nous. Enfin,

lo' dimansh d'abitud nu no' fezon pa gran-shoz
le dimanche d'habitude nous ne faisons pas grand-chose;

kelko' fwa per fe du brikolaj neseser
quelques fois, mon père fait du bricolage si nécessaire.

Translation

On Monday mornings, my father works at his office, my mother stays at the house, my little sister goes to school, and I go to university. On Tuesdays, Wednesdays, Thursdays and lastly Fridays, we do the same thing. But on weekends, it is quite different. During the weekend, we are not very busy like the other days. Saturday mornings, my father who is very athletic, goes swimming, and my mother cooks becaue every Saturday, my parents invite my aunt over for dinner with us. Finally, Sundays we usually don't do much. Sometimes my father does chores if necessary.

Notes

RRSM

FOR

JAPANESE USAGE GUIDELINES

It is becoming more popular among the new generation of the Japanese speaking to write its own language in accordance with English alphabet rules for ease in communication considering some degree of <u>approximate</u> pronunciations.

The presented English RRSM will improve this task for those who have some basic knowledge of English and Japanese languages

Japanese writing system is one of the more difficult Asian writing systems to learn and can be replaced with the English RRSM. See the following example to see how.

Notes

RRSM – JAPANESE USAGE – EXAMPLE 1

Risshun wo Sugite Higanagakunari

Haru
春
Yokino shitakara kusanomega kaowodashi
雪下から草の芽が顔を出し　立春を過ぎて日が長くなり
待ちに待った桜の季節を迎えます。　お花見を楽しみましょう。
Machinimatta sakurano Kisetsuwomukaemasu
Ohanamiwo Tanoshimimasho

Natsu
夏
Amaotoga Hibiku Baiuwasugoshi　Midori iyoiyo Fukakunatte
雨音が響く梅雨をすごし　緑いよいよ深くなって
暑さも本番。　海水浴に出かけましょう！
Atsusamo honban　Kaisuiyokuni Dekakemasho

Aki
秋
Hibikawaru Tsukinofuzeiha konokishetsu Naradahadesu
日々変わる月の風情はこの季節ならではです。
夜の空を見上げてみましょう。
Yorunosorawo　Miagetemimasho

Fayu
冬
Kiririto shitasamusa　Ichimenno Ginsekai
きりりとした寒さ　一面の銀世界。
白い清らかな世界がひろがります。
Shiroi kiyorakona　Sekaiga Hirogarimasu

新しい気持ちで新年を迎えましょう。
Atarashiikimochide　Shinnenwo mukaemasho.

Translation

The four beautiful seasons of Japan

Spring
　　The green grass peeking out of a blanket of snow,
　　And each day gets longer after Risshun, the first day of spring.
　　We meet the long-awaited cherry blossom season.
　　Let us enjoy hanami, the viewing of flowers.

Summer
　　Letting the rainy season pass along with the sound of the rain so slow,

　　Each day brings deeper and deeper greens
　　The summer heat has come.
　　Let's all go to the beach!

Autumn
　　The daily change in the moon's face makes the longing for autumn grow,

　　Let us look up into the night sky.

Winter
　　The crisp coldness over the snow
　　Fills the silvery world.
　　The clean and white world is the symbol of the season
　　Let us meet the New Year and start anew.

From the English learning program of Japan Broadcasting Corp.

Notes

RRSM

FOR

FARSI USAGE GUIDELINES

It is becoming more popular among the new generation of those who speak Farsi to write its own language in accordance with English alphabet rules for ease in communication considering some degree of approximate pronunciations.

The presented English RRSM will improve this task for those who have some basic knowledge of English and Farsi languages.

Farsi is a different language from Arabic, but it uses the difficult Arabic alphabet. This writing system can be replaced with the English RRSM as shown in the following example.

Notes

Kermanshah - Bazar

بازار ــ کرمانشاه

A'sil Va' A'sbhaye Gozashte Da'r Ast Iran Gha'rbe Da'r
A'sil Nejadeh Gozashte Da'r Ast Iran Gha'rbe Da'r Keshaverzi Moheme Az Marakeze Kermanshah

کرمانشاه از مراکز مهم کشاورزی در غرب ایران است. در گذشته اسبهای نژاده و اصیل

Sarboland Kordan Kordneshin Kermanshah Budeh Diyar
Va' Mardomani A'st Man'taghei A'st Za'banzad in

این دیار زبانزد بوده است. کرمانشاه منطقه‌ای کردنشین است. کردان مردمانی سربلند و

Bumi A'st Kohan Az Anan Ke
Kermanshahan Sanaye Irani Za'banhaye shakhei Za'bane Azadeh and

آزاده‌اند که زبان آنان شاخه‌ای از زبان‌های کهن ایرانی است. صنایع بومی کرمانشاهان

Bazare A'shayeri Farmuardehaye Kermanshahi Givehaye
Da'r Ghalihaye Va' cha'rmi Va' za'rife Manande

مانند گیوه‌های ظریف کرمانشاهی و فراورده‌های چرمی و قالی‌های عشایری در بازار

Bumi Shirinihaye Sayere Kak Berenji Misha'vad shahr Jonbo
Kermanshah Va' Va' Nane Arze Jushe Por

پرجنب‌وجوش شهر عرضه می‌شود. نان برنجی و کاک و سایر شیرینی‌های بومی کرمانشاه

Delpa'zir
A'st Besyar

بسیار دلپذیر است.

Translation:

Bazar of Kermanshah

Kermanshah is one of the important agricultural centers of west Iran. In the past, the original breed horses of this area was well known. Kermanshah is a Kurdish district populated with proud Kurds and their language is a branch of one of the ancient Iranian language. The native products of the Kermanshahians presented in this active crowded Bazar of the city are goods such as fancy comfort shoes, leather products, Ashayeri carpets, rice breads and various delicious local pastries.

Notes

REFERENCES

Recommended Web sites:

Interested readers can find support and more detailed information related to the subjects of this book at the following web sites.

1 - Ozideas Australian Centre for innovations / writing systems / word writing systems—an introduction

2 - History of English language

3 - Forms of English / Category: Forms of English

4 - Esperanto Language

5 - Turkish Language

6 - Albanian Language

7 - Azerbaijani Language

8 - French Pronunciations

9 - Spanish Pronunciations

Source of English examples:

Example 1. Nevada – From Travel Nevada & Leisure 2009 publication

Example 2. California – From AAA 2009 Northern California Tour Book

Example 3. Cabo San Lucas – From AAA 2009 Mexico Tour Book

Example 4. The Enjoyment of Music by Joseph Machlis. © 1955 by W. W. Norton & Company, Inc.

Example 5. "Well, at least the plate was blue" – From George Carlin's book *Napalm & Silly Putty*. © 2001 by Hyperion Publisher.

Example 6 & 7. More Wilderness & Modern Automobile – From *Reader Digest* magazine, September 2007.